# LIFEBOAT CREW MEMBER

### Rebecca Hunter

### Photography by Chris Fairclough

## CHERRYTREE BOOKS

A Cherrytree book

First published in 2008 by
Evans Brothers Ltd
2A Portman Mansions
Chiltern Street
London W1U 6NR

British Library Cataloguing in Publication Data
Hunter, Rebecca
  Lifeboat crew member - (People who help us)
  1. Lifeboat crew members - Juvenile literature
  I. Title
  363.1'2381

ISBN: 9781842345313

Planned and produced by Discovery Books Ltd
Editor: Rebecca Hunter
Designer: Ian Winton

**Acknowledgements**
Commissioned photography by Chris Fairclough.
Additional photography:  The following photographs were reproduced with kind permission of the RNLI:
p10 (bottom), p 11, p 20 (top and bottom), p 21 (top and bottom).

The author, packager and publisher would like to thank Graham Owen, Danielle Rush, Alun Owen,
Patrick Cheshire, Lucy Zalot, Jonathan Parry, Dave Jones, Richard and Oliver Williams-Bulkeley and
the Royal National Lifeboat Institution, for their help and participation in this book.

If you would like to find out more about the RNLI, visit their website at rnli.org.uk

Words appearing in red, **like this**, are explained in the glossary.

# Contents

# I am a lifeboat crew member

My name is Graham. I am a lifeboat crew member with the Royal National Lifeboat Institution (RNLI).

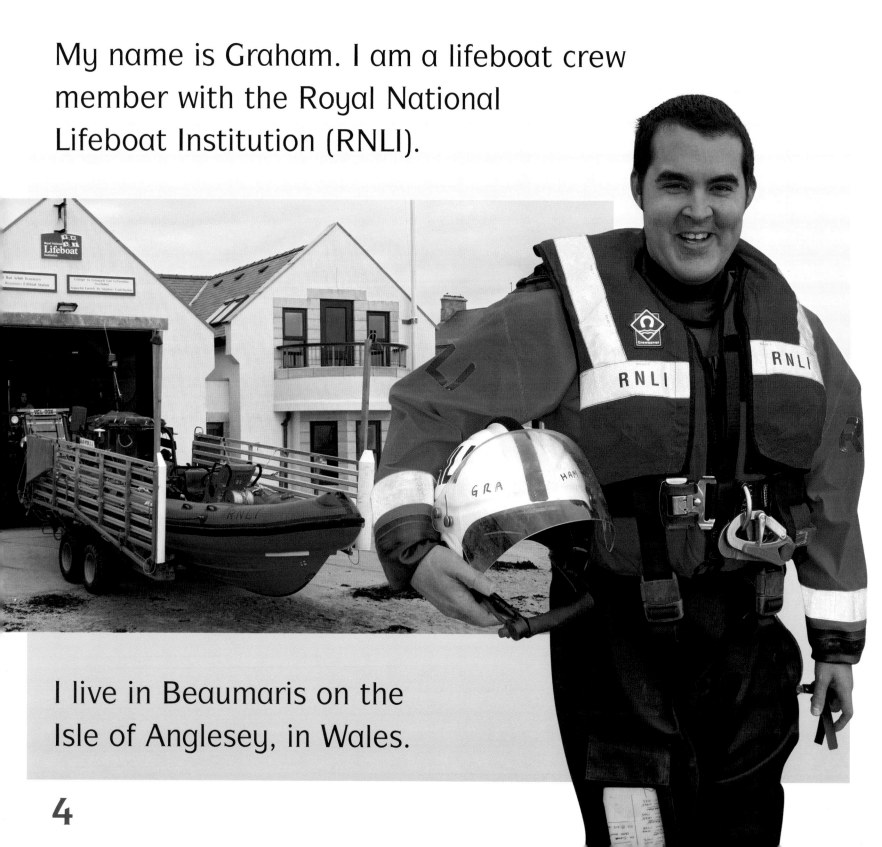

I live in Beaumaris on the Isle of Anglesey, in Wales.

The RNLI lifeboat service rescues people who are in trouble at sea. Lifeboat crew members have to be ready to help 24 hours a day.

**RNLI FACT**

A lifeboat like this costs £135,000.

The RNLI has over 330 lifeboats.

Royal National **Lifeboat** Institution

Supported Entirely By Voluntary Contributions

**BLUE PETER II**

**BEAUMARIS LIFEBOAT STATION**

Our boat was bought with money raised by the children's television programme 'Blue Peter'.

# My job

I do not get paid for being a lifeboat crew member. I am a **volunteer**.

ABC
Power Marine

Chandlery
Boat &
Engine Sales
Servicing
Tel. 01248 811413

Most crew members have other jobs that they are paid to do. I work at a marine **chandlery** shop.

The shop sells boating equipment, like rope and lifejackets.

Dave owns a **charter boat** and has come in to buy some rope. I know him well because he is also a member of the lifeboat crew.

## Contacting the RNLI

If you see someone in trouble on a boat or in the water, you should call 999 and ask for the coastguard. If they decide a lifeboat is needed, they will contact the RNLI. The lifeboat crew will be called to help on their pagers (above). I always carry my pager with me. Even if I am at work I can be at the lifeboat station within 5 minutes.

# Training day

Today some of the lifeboat crew are meeting at the lifeboat station to do some training.

Alun is an **electrician** who helps launch the lifeboat. Lucy is a teacher and Jonathan has a car cleaning business.

We plan the afternoon. We are expecting some visitors. Then we are going to launch the lifeboat and practise a 'man overboard' drill.

# A new recruit

Richard is visiting our station today. He is interested in joining the lifeboat crew.

If Richard joins us, he will have special training at the Lifeboat College in Poole, Dorset.

This picture shows trainees doing a **capsize** drill in the college's wave pool. It is important to know how to get a boat upright again after a capsize.

# Donating money

Today two brothers have come to visit us. Last month Oliver got into trouble on his windsurf board.

A lifeboat brought him back to the shore. It was lucky his friends knew who to call.

I show the boys around the lifeboat.

Oliver was very grateful that the RNLI was able to help him. He decided to thank us by raising some money at his school.

The boys present a cheque for one thousand pounds to to Patrick, our fundraising manager. We have our photos taken with Stormy Stan, our **mascot**.

The RNLI relies on **donations** like this to keep going. It is a **charity**.

# The launch

Now it is time to launch the lifeboat. I collect my kit from the locker room.

I wear an inner thermal suit and an outer dry suit. On top of this I have to wear yellow boots, gloves, a helmet and a lifejacket.

## RNLI FACT

Crew kit costs

Gloves  £16

Yellow boots  £40

All-weather lifejacket  £500

Our lifeboat is 7 metres long and launches from a tractor-driven carriage.

Alun drives it down to the water.

The lifeboat has three volunteers on board. I am the **helmsman**. When we are in deep enough water, I start the engines and drive off.

# Man overboard!

We head out into deeper water to do the 'man overboard' drill.

We drop the **dummy** overboard and circle round to pick it up.

I have to steer the boat carefully into the right position so we can rescue the dummy.

Lucy and Jonathan pull it back on board. It is important to practise this drill, so that we can rescue real people quickly and safely.

**RNLI FACT**
There are about 23 real lifeboat launches every day of the year.

Now we can return to the station.

# Returning the lifeboat

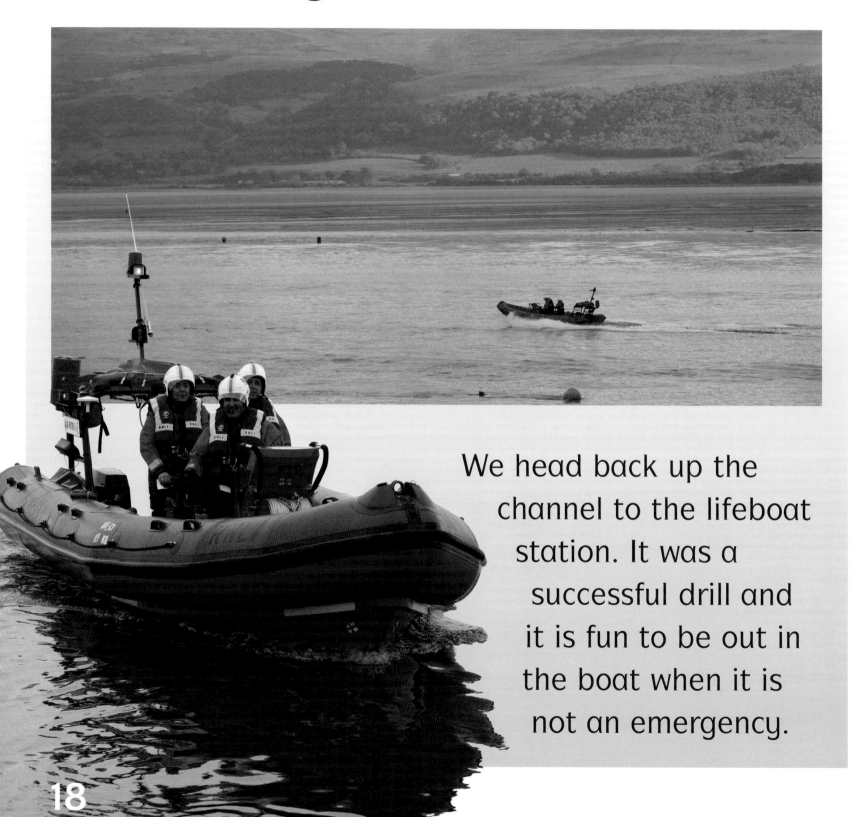

We head back up the channel to the lifeboat station. It was a successful drill and it is fun to be out in the boat when it is not an emergency.

I drive onto the lifeboat carriage and Alun brings the boat back up the beach.

We hose down the boat, trailer and tractor with fresh water. Salty seawater makes metal rust, so we must wash away every trace of it. Finally we refuel the lifeboat so it is ready to go again, and put it back in the boathouse.

# Lifeboat rescues

The RNLI is on call every day of the year and covers the coastline all around the country.

Here an inshore lifeboat (right) helps a group of teenagers who were stranded on a beach after being cut off by the tide.

This lifeboat crew is helping a child who was washed out to sea on an **inflatable** dinghy.

This 10-year-old boy was watching seals on the rocks when he became cut off by the tide.

Sometimes the lifeboat crew members are assisted by a helicopter. Here, a **winchman** from the helicopter is being lowered onto the lifeboat.

# Lifeboat guild

Back at the station some women from the local lifeboat guild have come to talk to Patrick and me. They are in charge of raising funds to keep the RNLI going in our area.

It is time for me to go home.

My last task of the day is to shut the door of the boathouse. I am very proud to be part of the RNLI's lifeboat rescue service.

**RNLI FACT**

It costs about £335,000 a day to run the whole of the RNLI.

# Glossary

**capsize**  to turn upside down

**chandlery**  a shop that sells supplies and equipment for boats

**charity**  an organization set up to provide help and raise money for those in need

**charter boat**  a boat that is available for hire

**donation**  something that is given to a charity

**dummy**  a lifesize model of a person

**electrician**  a person who installs and maintains electrical equipment

**helmsman**  a person who steers a ship or boat

**inflatable**  something that can be filled with air

**mascot**  something that is supposed to bring good luck

**volunteer**  a person who works for an organization without being paid

**winchman**  a person who operates a winch

# Index